I CAN DO IT!

I CAN USE A DICTIONARY

by Susan Ashley

Photographs by Gregg Andersen

Reading consultant: Susan Nations, M.Ed., author/literacy coach/consultant

WEEKLY WR READER®
EARLY LEARNING LIBRARY

Please visit our web site at: www.earlyliteracy.cc
For a free color catalog describing Weekly Reader® Early Learning Library's
list of high-quality books, call 1-877-445-5824 (USA) or 1-800-387-3178 (Canada).
Weekly Reader® Early Learning Library's fax: (414) 336-0164.

Library of Congress Cataloging-in-Publication Data

Ashley, Susan.
   I can use a dictionary / by Susan Ashley.
     p. cm. — (I can do it!)
   Includes bibliographical references and index.
   ISBN 0-8368-4326-6 (lib. bdg.)
   ISBN 0-8368-4333-9 (softcover)
   1. English language—Dictionaries—Juvenile literature. 2. Encyclopedias
and dictionaries—Juvenile literature. I. Title. II. I can do it! (Milwaukee, Wis.)
PE1611.A84 2004
423—dc22
                                           2004045130

This edition first published in 2005 by
Weekly Reader® Early Learning Library
330 West Olive Street, Suite 100
Milwaukee, WI 53212 USA

Copyright © 2005 by Weekly Reader® Early Learning Library

Editor: JoAnn Early Macken
Graphic Designer: Melissa Valuch
Art Director: Tammy West
Picture Researcher: Diane Laska-Swanke
Photographer: Gregg Andersen

Printed in the United States of America

1 2 3 4 5 6 7 8 9 08 07 06 05 04

Note to Educators and Parents

Reading is such an exciting adventure for young children! They are beginning to integrate their oral language skills with written language. To encourage children along the path to early literacy, books must be colorful, engaging, and interesting; they should invite the young reader to explore both the print and the pictures.

I Can Do It! is a new series designed to help young readers learn how ordinary children reach everyday goals. Each book describes a different task that any child can be proud to accomplish.

Each book is specially designed to support the young reader in the reading process. The familiar topics are appealing to young children and invite them to read — and re-read — again and again. The full-color photographs and enhanced text further support the student during the reading process.

In addition to serving as wonderful picture books in schools, libraries, homes, and other places where children learn to love reading, these books are specifically intended to be read within an instructional guided reading group. This small group setting allows beginning readers to work with a fluent adult model as they make meaning from the text. After children develop fluency with the text and content, the book can be read independently. Children and adults alike will find these books supportive, engaging, and fun!

— Susan Nations, M.Ed., author, literacy coach, and consultant in literacy development

I can use a dictionary. A dictionary helps me learn about words.

Our classroom has a dictionary. My teacher can help me find it.

FIRST FUN DICTIONARY

more than 1,000 carefully chosen entries
more than 500 illustrations and photographs
word game and puzzles

DICTIONARY

Cindy Leaney

A dictionary is full of words. The words are listed in order from A to Z.

A
B
C
D
E
F
G
H
I
J
K
L
M
N
O
P
Q
R
S
T

elec·tron \i-'lek-,trän\ *n*
a very small particle that has a
negative charge of electricity and
travels around the nucleus of an
atom

elec·tron·ic \i-,lek-'trän-ik\ *adj*
1 of, relating to, or using the
principles of electronics
⟨an *electronic* device⟩
2 operating by means of or
using an electronic device (as
a computer) ⟨an *electronic*
typewriter⟩ ⟨*electronic* banking⟩
elec·tron·i·cal·ly *adv*

electronic mail *n*
E-MAIL

elec·tron·ics \i-,lek-'trän-iks\ *n*
a science that deals with the giving
off, action, and effects of electrons
in vacuums, gases, and
semiconductors and with devices
using such electrons

electron tube *n*
a device in which conduction of
electricity by electrons takes place
through a vacuum or a gas within
a sealed container and which has
various uses (as in radio and
television)

elec·tro·scope \i-'lek-trə-,skōp\ *n*
an instrument for discovering the
presence of an electric charge on
a body and for finding out whether
the charge is positive or negative

el·e·gance \'el-i-gəns\ *n*
1 refined gracefulness
2 decoration that is rich but in
good taste

el·e·gant \'el-i-gənt\ *adj*
showing good taste (as in dress or
manners) : having or showing
beauty and refinement
el·e·gant·ly *adv*

el·e·gy \'el-ə-jē\ *n, pl* **el·e·gies**
a sad or mournful poem usually
expressing sorrow for one who is
dead

elephant

The African and the Indian elephant are the largest land animals
on earth, and the last two living species of a group of animals
with a long, flexible snout. Elephants are intelligent and sociable
creatures. Females and calves live in family herds, led by an older
female, while males past puberty form their own herds or travel
alone. Elephants feed on vegetation such as grass and leaves.

concave back

large ear

flat
forehead

tusk

features
an African
elephant

convex back

smaller ear

twin-domed
forehead

9

features
an India

I use a dictionary
when I write.

It shows me how to spell a word. I am looking up the word "orchard."

or·chard \'òr-chərd\ *n*
  1 a place where fruit trees are grown
  2 the trees in an orchard
or·ches·tra \'òr-kə-strə\ *n*
  1 a group of musicians who perform instrumental music using mostly stringed instruments

I use a dictionary
when I read.

It shows me how
to say a word.

adj
that can be recycled ⟨*recyclab*
plastic bottles⟩
re·cy·cle \'rē-'sī-kəl\ *vb*
re·cy·cled; **re·cy·cling**
▶ to process
⟨as paper,

glass bottle —

A dictionary gives
me a definition.
A definition is the
meaning of a word.

re·cy·cla·ble \(ˌ)rē-'sī-kə-lə-bəl\
adj
that can be recycled ⟨*recyclable* plastic bottles⟩

re·cy·cle \'rē-'sī-kəl\ *vb*
re·cy·cled;
re·cy·cling
▶ to process (as paper, glass, or cans) in order to regain materials for human use

glass bottle

19

Here is a new word.
What does it mean?
I will look it up!

Glossary

definition — the meaning of a word

order — one after another

spell — to name or write the letters of a word in order

For More Information

Books

Collins First School Dictionary. Marie Lister and Jock Graham (HarperCollins)

Collins First School Dictionary Skills. Anita Scholes and Barry Scholes (HarperCollins)

My First Visual Dictionary/Mi Primer Diccionario Visual. (Gareth Stevens)

Scholastic Visual Dictionary. Jean-Claude Corbeil and Ariane Archambault (Scholastic)

Web Sites

Little Explorers English Picture Dictionary
www.enchantedlearning.com/Dictionary.html
Online dictionary with pictures and definitions

Index

classroom 6
definitions 18
learning 4
looking up 12, 20
reading 14

saying 16
spelling 12
teacher 6
writing 10

About the Author

Susan Ashley has written more than twenty-five books for children. She has lived all over the United States and in Europe. Thanks to her travels, she has become very good at reading maps and writing letters. She also likes making — and eating — sandwiches. Susan lives in Wisconsin with her husband and two cats. The cats like it when she makes tuna sandwiches!